INDIA IN AFRICA: IMPLICATIONS OF AN EMERGING POWER FOR AFRICOM AND U.S. STRATEGY

J. Peter Pham

March 2011

*****

Comments pertaining to this report are invited and should be forwarded to: Director, Strategic Studies Institute, U.S. Army War College, 122 Forbes Ave, Carlisle, PA 17013-5244.

*****

All Strategic Studies Institute (SSI) publications may be downloaded free of charge from the SSI website. Hard copies of this report may also be obtained free of charge while supplies last by placing an order on the SSI website. The SSI website address is: *www.StrategicStudiesInstitute.army.mil.*

*****

The Strategic Studies Institute publishes a monthly e-mail newsletter to update the national security community on the research of our analysts, recent and forthcoming publications, and upcoming conferences sponsored by the Institute. Each newsletter also provides a strategic commentary by one of our research analysts. If you are interested in receiving this newsletter, please subscribe on the SSI website at *www.StrategicStudiesInstitute. army.mil/newsletter/.*

FOREWORD

Several trends make this monograph topic important. First, Africa, long marginalized in international relations, has emerged today as a strategically, diplomatically, and economically vital component in the global balance of the 21st century, with the major powers seeking access to the continent's resources and forging ties with African governments and peoples. The establishment of the United States Africa Command (AFRICOM) is but one indication of America's growing network of political, economic, and security commitments in Africa. Second, the United States is also actively seeking to build a strong strategic partnership with India, a country whose rapid economic growth, geopolitical position, and proven commitment to democracy make it an especially attractive ally not just in South Asia, but more broadly. Third, as it continues its rise to global power status, India is cultivating its own expanding set of relations across the African continent—a phenomenon that is nowhere as well known as the increasing penetration there of the People's Republic of China.

In this monograph, Dr. J. Peter Pham provides a framework for understanding both India's approach to Africa, especially in the military and security sector, and the responses of Africans to it. He also argues that the United States should engage India in Africa, both as an end in itself and within the context of broader U.S.-India ties. What emerges from this analysis is a call to both greater mutual awareness and concrete bilateral cooperation that would not only positively benefit the two countries, but also redound to the advantage of their African allies.

DOUGLAS C. LOVELACE, JR.
Director
Strategic Studies Institute

ABOUT THE AUTHOR

J. PETER PHAM is Director of the Michael S. Ansari Africa Center at the Atlantic Council of the United States. In addition, Dr. Pham holds an academic appointment as tenured Associate Professor of Justice Studies, Political Science, and African Studies at James Madison University, and regularly lectures at the Foreign Service Institute, the Joint Special Operations University, the Defense Institute of Security Assistance Management, and other U.S. Government professional educational institutions. Dr. Pham has testified before the U.S. Congress on a number of occasions and conducted briefings or consulted for U.S. and foreign governments as well as private firms. In May 2008, at the invitation of General William E. "Kip" Ward, he gave the keynote address at the first Senior Leaders Conference of the United States Africa Command (AFRICOM) in Mainz, Germany. He currently serves on AFRICOM's Senior Advisory Group. Dr. Pham is the incumbent Vice President of the Association for the Study of the Middle East and Africa (ASMEA), an academic organization chaired by Professor Bernard Lewis, which represents over 1,000 scholars of Middle Eastern and African Studies at more than 300 colleges and universities in the United States and overseas. He is also Editor-in-Chief of ASMEA's flagship *Journal of the Middle East and Africa*. A specialist on U.S. foreign and defense policy, African politics and security, and terrorism and political violence, Dr. Pham is the author of over 300 essays and reviews. He is the author, editor, or translator of over a dozen books and regularly appears in numerous national and international media outlets.

SUMMARY

The U.S. Africa Command (AFRICOM) — whose mission, "in concert with other U.S. government agencies and international partners," is to conduct "sustained security engagement through military-to-military programs, military-sponsored activities, and other military operations as directed to promote a stable and secure African environment"[1] — is not alone in recognizing the strategic importance of Africa. This continent, in fact, has increasingly attracted significant attention from the major powers. While the extensive network of economic, political, and military ties that the People's Republic of China (PRC) has constructed across Africa in recent years, is relatively well known, India's own rapidly expanding network of connections to the continent have gone largely unexamined.

In fact, Indo-African ties are of long standing, arising from a unique historical experience that stretches from pre-colonial trade patterns through modern India's generous financial and diplomatic support for African liberation movements in the late 20th century. Motivating the country's current activities in Africa is its quests for resources, business opportunities, diplomatic influence, and security. Of particular note is the significant investment that India has made in African security, reflected in both support for and participation in United Nations (UN) peacekeeping operations, and providing a selective security umbrella today and training for some of the African military leaders of tomorrow.

What is the impact of all this on Africa? First, there is no doubt that Africa stands to benefit from the addition of India to the list of countries seeking access to the continent's natural resources and markets, as well as political and strategic partnerships with African states. Second, in general it could be said that India's approach, with its emphasis not just on trade, but also training and infrastructure development, benefits Africans. Third, India's long-standing commitment to secularism, pluralism, and democracy, and the lessons it learned while freeing itself from the constraints imposed by its longtime oppressively low rate of economic growth, are precisely what many African states ought to emulate. Fourth, overall, the burgeoning Indian-African relationship presents good prospects for security and stability in Africa; in fact, India's history enables its government to speak authoritatively on issues like terrorism in many places where, quite simply, the credibility of the United States and some of its allies may be somewhat limited.

India is not likely to present a direct challenge to the core interests of the United States in what U.S. policymakers and analysts now recognize to be the geostrategically vital region of Sub-Saharan Africa. Moreover, many of India's national interests—like maintaining peace and security along the Indian Ocean littoral, including the eastern coast of Africa—align quite well with America's broader military and strategic interests in the same area. Thus, the United States ought to view the prospering Indian-African relationship positively.

From an American perspective, what steps might American leaders take to enhance the U.S.-Indian relationship overall and foster cooperation in Africa that advances both countries' interests in promoting good governance, supporting economic growth and development, increasing access to health and educational resources, and helping to prevent, mitigate, and resolve conflicts on the continent?

- First, reaffirm explicitly the U.S. commitment to facilitate India's rise to major power status.
- Second, recognize that, especially in Africa, U.S. interests would be well served by India's involvement in bilateral and multilateral security initiatives with its African partners.
- Third, ensure that AFRICOM and other U.S. institutions develop the appropriate mechanisms with which to engage and, where appropriate, to partner with Indian forces serving with UN peacekeeping missions and other Indian security initiatives in Africa.

In short, the willingness of New Delhi to commit to peacekeeping, peace enforcement, and nation-building efforts that Washington has largely lacked either the political will or the resources to engage in on the continent, not only complements U.S. efforts to promote greater stability and security in Africa but, by providing an opportunity for substantive bilateral cooperation, can also contribute directly to strengthening the emergent Indo-American strategic partnership.

ENDNOTE

1. U.S. Africa Command, Fact Sheet, "United States Africa Command," October 18, 2008, available from *www.africom.mil/getArticle.asp?art=1644*.

INDIA IN AFRICA: IMPLICATIONS OF AN EMERGING POWER FOR AFRICOM AND U.S. STRATEGY

Introduction.

On July 11, 2009, President Barack Obama addressed the Parliament of Ghana during his first visit to Sub-Saharan Africa since his election. In this speech, the President affirmed that "Africa's future is up to Africans"[1] and consequently that they had to take the responsibility:

> Now, it's easy to point fingers and to pin the blame of these problems on others. Yes, a colonial map that made little sense helped to breed conflict. The West has often approached Africa as a patron or a source of resources rather than a partner. But the West is not responsible for the destruction of the Zimbabwean economy over the last decade, or wars in which children are enlisted as combatants. In my father's life, it was partly tribalism and patronage and nepotism in an independent Kenya that for a long stretch derailed his career, and we know that this kind of corruption is still a daily fact of life for far too many. . . .

> Development depends on good governance. That is the ingredient which has been missing in far too many places, for far too long. That's the change that can unlock Africa's potential. And that is a responsibility that can only be met by Africans.[2]

Nevertheless, the President went on to list four critical areas—building and sustaining democratic governments, supporting development that provides opportunity to more people, strengthening public health, and resolving conflicts peacefully—for which he pledged America's support:

1

As for America and the West, our commitment must be measured by more than just the dollars we spend. I've pledged substantial increases in our foreign assistance, which is in Africa's interests and America's interests. But the true sign of success is not whether we are a source of perpetual aid that helps people scrape by — it's whether we are partners in building the capacity for transformational change.

Moreover, the President went on to explain that it was in the interests of the United States to assist Africa's development, even if responsible government were a condition for the aid:

This is the simple truth of a time when the boundaries between people are overwhelmed by our connections. Your prosperity can expand America's prosperity. Your health and security can contribute to the world's health and security. And the strength of your democracy can help advance human rights for people everywhere. So I do not see the countries and peoples of Africa as a world apart; I see Africa as a fundamental part of our interconnected world — as partners with America on behalf of the future we want for all of our children.[3]

The administration has acted on this guidance, maintaining and, in some instances, expanding many of the previously undertaken development and humanitarian initiatives — including the Millennium Challenge Corporation (MCC), the President's Emergency Plan for AIDS Relief (PEPFAR), and the President's Malaria Initiative (PMI) — that have positively demonstrated American commitment to Africa and strengthened the "soft power" links between the United States and the nations of the African continent. Funding has also modestly increased for the U.S. Africa Command (AFRICOM), whose mission, "in concert with other U.S. government agencies and international partners," is to conduct "sustained security engagement through military-to-military programs, military-sponsored activities, and other military operations as directed to promote a stable and secure African environment."[4] This represents America's recognition of the security and strategic importance of Africa, impacting not only Africans but the interests of the United States and the international community as a whole.

Less than 5 days after the President delivered the words above, Indian Prime Minister Manmohan Singh took to the podium during the Fifteenth Summit of the Non-Aligned Movement (NAM) in Sharm-el-Sheikh, Egypt, to declare:

> Nowhere are the challenges humankind faces more pressing than in the continent of Africa. NAM should work to give Africa's problems, and equally its prospects, pre-eminence in the global development agenda. Making Africa an active participant in global economic processes is a moral imperative. It also makes good economic sense. India is committed to develop a comprehensive partnership with Africa. As a first step, we held the first India-Africa Forum Summit in New Delhi in 2008. We are ready to work with other NAM countries to enhance our partnership in areas that are of priority to Africa.[5]

The extensive network of economic, political, and military ties that the People's Republic of China (PRC) has constructed across Africa in recent years has been the subject of increased scrutiny on the part of African policymakers, businesspeople, scholars, and activists, as well as their counterparts in the United States, Europe, and elsewhere[6] — including several insightful studies of the strategic implications of the hitherto modest, but nonetheless significant, presence of Chinese military forces and other security-related engagements.[7] However, India's rapidly expanding network of relations on the continent have gone largely unexamined, with the exception of a small number of relatively short essays.[8] Moreover, this limited body of literature has treated the military dimension, at best, only in passing. But as Africa, long marginalized in international relations, becomes increasingly recognized as strategically, diplomatically, and economically vital to both the emerging 21st century global order and the individual national interests of the major powers, India's burgeoning public and private investments in the region as well as its policies vis-à-vis African regional organizations and individual states need to be better understood. This is especially true of U.S. policymakers and others responsible for managing America's own growing political, economic, and security commitments on the continent. Only thus can it be possible to consider ways to engage India in Africa, both as an end in itself and within the context of broader U.S.-India ties.[9]

India and Africa: History.

While to a certain extent New Delhi's approach to Africa can be viewed as driven by many of the same motivations as Beijing's better-known efforts — including the quests for resources, business opportunities, diplomatic influence, and security — there is a need first for an appreciation of the unique historical experience that shaped the contours of and continues to influence the ongoing development of Indo-African relations.

Contacts between India and Africa date back to ancient times, with Indian merchants conducting relatively extensive trade along the eastern littoral of the African continent—a point recalled when one leading Indian strategist, C. Raja Mohan, who served on his country's National Security Advisory Board, describes India's "near abroad" as including "parts of Africa, the Persian Gulf, Central and Southeast Asia, and the Indian Ocean region" in that order.[10] Likewise, the late historian Basil Davidson noted: "What the Phoenician-Berber connection had achieved in northwestern Africa . . . the traders and mariners of Greek-ruled Egypt, southern Arabia, East Africa, and India largely repeated in the last centuries before the Christian era. By then the steady winds of the western half of the Indian Ocean, blowing back and forth between West India and East Africa in regular seasonal variation, were used by sailors who had learned how to trim their sails."[11]

The period of European colonial expansion brought an end to this long-range trading system. On the other hand, the incorporation of both the Indian subcontinent and large swaths of Africa into the British Empire facilitated the establishment of substantial communities of people of Indian origin in Africa.[12] No less a figure than Mohandas K. (Mahatma) Gandhi, the future father of Indian independence, was part of this movement, accepting a position with an Indian law firm in Natal in 1893 and remaining in South Africa until 1914, a period during which his leadership of the Indian community's struggle for civil rights saw the first flowering of what would become his hallmark approach of *Satyagraha*, or nonviolent resistance to tyranny. In turn, Gandhi's philosophy, which he successfully put into practice to achieve India's independence in 1947, was to inspire a generation of African leaders—including Kwame Nkrumah of Ghana, Obafemi Awolowo of Nigeria, Julius Nyerere of Tanzania, and Kenneth Kaunda of Zambia—in their own national liberation campaigns.[13]

It bears recording that when India became independent, there were only four sovereign states in all of Africa: Egypt, Ethiopia, Liberia, and South Africa. India quickly established diplomatic relations with the first two, while it had difficulty with South Africa due to the latter country's treatment of persons of Indian origin. For the other countries of Africa, especially those under British colonial rule, India availed itself of its privilege as a member of the Commonwealth to post commissioners, often also accredited as consuls-general, who not only looked after the interests of their fellow citizens but also established ties with local African leaders. In fact, the first Indian commissioner in British East Africa, the Nairobi-based Apasaheb Balasaheb Pant, was so supportive of the nationalist aspirations of the African population that the colonial authorities demanded his recall. The solicitude of diplomats like Pant and his Accra-based counterpart for British West Africa was appreciated by the leaders of the eventually independent African states. After Ghana gained independence, for example, one of Nkrumah's first forays overseas was an official visit to India and, while Ghana was still getting its foreign service organized, the West African country entrusted the protection of its political interests in the Middle East to the Indian diplomatic legations in Egypt, Saudi Arabia, and Syria.

If Mahatma Gandhi laid the moral foundations for Indo-African relations, it was Jawaharlal Nehru who gave the relationship its political structure during his long tenure as India's first prime minister (1947-64). He declared that Africa, though separated by the Indian Ocean from us, is effectively "our next door neighbor" and that "in historical perspective, Indian interests are likely to be bound up more and more with the growth of Africa."[14] Moreover, Nehru pursued a policy of supporting African national struggles against colonialism as well as against apartheid in South Africa. Together with China's Zhou Enlai, Egypt's Gamal Abdel Nasser, Ghana's Nkrumah, Indonesia's Sukarno, and Vietnam's Ho Chi Minh, Nehru played a leading role in convening the first Asian-African Conference, which brought together representatives of 29 African and Asian countries in the Indonesian city of Bandung, giving rise to the Non-Aligned Movement (NAM).[15] Unlike the PRC, which hoped to use the NAM to advance Mao Zedong's revolutionary ambitions worldwide, or Egypt, which saw it as a vehicle for promoting Nasser's pan-Arabism in the Middle East, India's nationalist leaders were intently committed to blazing a truly independent path in international relations. As Nehru wrote on the eve of India's independence, "India could not be a mere hanger-on of any country or group of nations; her freedom and growth would make a vital difference to Asia and therefore to the world."[16]

However, early hopes of a more intensive Indo-African partnership were dashed when China and India came to blows over border disputes and the Sino-Indian War of 1962 left the PRC in possession of the contested areas. The result was not only a setback for India's standing among the NAM nations (only Egypt stood firmly behind India), but also led policymakers in New Delhi to adopt a less ambitious national policy, focusing instead on building their country's defense sector and securing its immediate neighborhood. (In contrast, at least until the Cultural Revolution decimated the ranks of their experienced diplomats, the Sino-Soviet schism gave leaders in Beijing added impetus to pursue engagements with the "nonaligned" countries of Sub-Saharan Africa so as to counter the ideological influence of their rivals in Moscow.[17])

Nonetheless, India continued to generously support national liberation movements in Africa, both financially and politically. New Delhi even accorded formal diplomatic recognition to South Africa's African National Congress (ANC) in 1967 and future Namibia's South West African People's Organization (SWAPO) in 1985 during the premierships, respectively, of Pandit Nehru's daughter, Indira Gandhi, and his grandson, Rajiv Gandhi. During the 1970s and 1980s, India provided both liberation movements with material and technical support. At the Eighth NAM Summit in Harare, Zimbabwe, in 1986, Rajiv Gandhi was chiefly responsible for the establishment of the Action for Resisting Invasion, Colonialism, and Apartheid (AFRICA) Fund to aid the "frontline" states in supporting the victims of apartheid and was elected as its first chairman. India contributed $40 million of the Fund's initial capital of $70 million.[18]

Even if official Indian policy paid less attention to Africa, however, it should be noted that the India diaspora was always present on the continent and played an important part in the economic life of the countries where they settled. In some cases, they were victims of their own success, attracting the malevolent attention of despots like Uganda's Idi Amin who found them useful scapegoats for an economy wrecked by his squandering on military hardware and personnel and, in 1972, ordered the expulsion of an estimated 45,000 individuals of South Asian descent—thus tragically

collapsing what remained of his economy.[19] Nevertheless, through time and the vicissitudes it brought, these
communities endured as a bridgehead for Indian interests—cultural, economic, and political—in Africa.
The former Indian foreign secretary, Salman Haidar,
for example, has even hailed the *felix culpa* (fortunate
blame) that people of Indian origin endured: they
"went through the constraints and indignities of the
apartheid era and joined in the fight against it." Now,
as he noted on the occasion of a visit several years ago
by External Affairs Minister Pranab Mukherjee to the
Africa Union, "their ties with the mother country are
strengthening and they can be regarded as a significant base for expansion of trade and commerce."[20]

In short, India's foreign policy during much of the
Cold War did not have significant direct impact on
the unfolding of developments in Africa. However,
India's political commitment to the NAM and its at
least rhetorical emphasis on South-South cooperation,
especially coupled with its consistent diplomatic support for African nationalist movements, still left India
well positioned to take up its engagements across the
continent and forge new ties, as it has done in recent
years. One researcher at the Institute for Defense and
Strategic Analysis, a think tank funded by the Indian
Ministry of Defense, has even laid out a succinct road
map for such a policy:

> The people of Africa have acknowledged India's sup-
> port in the past and there is a lot of goodwill towards
> India. They are attracted towards the image of India in
> the 21st century as the new center for technology and
> commerce in Asia.

India should reciprocate and follow the EU and the Japanese examples for cooperation to mutual benefit. Economically, this partnership with Africa would entail working closely with Africa on [the New Partnership for Africa's Development, NEPAD]. Culturally, it would entail greater interaction with people of Indian origin in Africa. Similarly, it involves the task of bringing Africa closer to the people of India through events like the Festival of Africa in India. Educationally, it would involve greater bilateral interaction between the two regions at all levels — school, college and university. Internally, it should lead to popularizing African studies in our country. Diplomatically, it should involve looking at ways and means to garner support for India's strategic interests.[21]

India's Quest for Natural Resources.

India's economy is projected to grow at a rate of somewhere between 8 and 10 percent annually over the next 2 decades[22] and is the only major economy predicted to record growth rates significantly above 3 percent by 2050.[23] The country, home of the world's fourth-largest national economy, became a trillion-dollar economy in early 2008.[24] The country's population of more than 1.1 billion accounts for one-sixth of humanity, with more than half of Indians under the age of 24.9, compared to the rapidly aging populations in other major countries, including China.[25] Despite the dynamism that these data imply, with its proven petroleum reserves remaining stagnant at less than 0.5 percent of the world total, India faces a potentially serious energy crisis. Currently the country is the fifth largest consumer of energy in the world, accounting for some 3.7 percent of the total global consumption. A third of India's energy needs, moreover, are presently met by traditional sources of fuel, including

10

wood, dung, crop residue, and waste. However, with increased development, India is expected to double its energy consumption by 2030, overtaking Japan and Russia in the process to become the world's third largest consumer (after the United States and China) — and these new needs can hardly be expected to be met by recourse to the traditional sources hitherto used by many households on the subcontinent.[26]

According to data from the International Energy Agency, India currently imports about 75 percent of its oil, a foreign dependence projected to rise to over 90 percent by 2020.[27] Given that most of these imports are coming from the volatile Middle East, where political conditions can easily give rise to sporadic disruptions that would jeopardize the country's economic security, it is more than understandable that India would seek an alternative supply of energy in the burgeoning African oil sector. Thus, for example, the Oil and Natural Gas Corporation (ONGC) Videsh (OVL), the overseas division of India's state-owned ONGC, has aggressively sought stakes in exploration and development across the continent.

In 2005, teaming up with the world's largest steel maker, Mittal (now Arcelor Mittal), owned by London-based Indian billionaire Lakshmi Mittal, OVL formed a new entity, ONGC Mittal Energy Ltd. (OMEL), which agreed to a $6 billion infrastructure deal with Nigeria in exchange for extensive access to some of the best oil production blocks in the West African country. More controversially, in 2006, OVL also plunked down $690 million to acquire a 25-percent stake in Sudan's Greater Nile Oil Project, despite the resistance of the China National Petroleum Corporation (CNPC), which has a 40-percent ownership in the enterprise. OVL subsequently acquired minority interests in two other oil blocks in Sudan, although the subsequent laggard implementation of the Comprehensive Peace Agreement between the regime in Khartoum and the Sudan People's Liberation Army/Movement as well as the ongoing humanitarian crisis in Darfur—to say nothing of the lack of democracy and good governance in Sudan as a whole—have posed challenges to Indian interests there.[28]

Meanwhile another Indian state-owned entity, the India Oil Corporation (IOC), has invested $1 billion in an offshore block in Côte d'Ivoire. ONGC has obtained permission to conduct geological studies in the exclusive economic zone of Mauritius. Other African countries being courted by Indian oil companies include Burkina Faso, Equatorial Guinea, Ghana, Guinea-Bissau, and Senegal. In 2009, ONGC Videsh initiated a bid to buy U.S.-based Kosmos Energy's 30-percent stake in Ghana's offshore Jubilee oilfield. The deal, although ultimately not consummated, would have cost between $3 billion and $4 billion.[29] In total, Africa currently accounts for about 20 percent of India's oil imports, a figure that will only rise in coming years. Not surprisingly, energy researchers have found that "India has focused development lending initiatives on the resource-rich countries of West Africa whose [national oil companies] are keen to gain deals."[30]

It should be noted, however, that unlike China and a number of other countries with which it in competition for access to Africa's petroleum resources, India has "stressed that it [is] interested not just in buying Africa's oil but in participating in all phases of oil production, refining, storage, and transport."[31] That message has found resonance with African countries like Uganda, which is beginning to exploit an estimated 2-billion-barrel petroleum reserve in the Albertine Rift region. In early 2010, Ugandan Vice President Gilbert Balibaseka Bukenya asked India for assistance to more quickly develop his country's oil and natural gas sector, explicitly appealing to ONGC and IOC for "simple and inexpensive means" for "accelerating development of different areas along the hydrocarbon value chain."[32] India has adopted that same comprehensive approach in its pursuit of access to Nigeria's hydrocarbon resources where it is in direct competition with Chinese interests. In early 2010, Indian Petroleum and Natural Gas Minister Murli Deora traveled to Nigeria to highlight Indian firms' willingness to participate in the West African country's nascent master plan for gas development, especially in the construction of petrochemical plants, liquefied natural gas (LNG), and LNG pipelines.[33]

Hydrocarbons are not the only natural resources being sought by the growing Indian economy. Vedanta Resources, a publicly traded metals conglomerate founded in Mumbai in 1976, has invested over $750 million in Zambian copper mines, while Liberia entered into a 25-year deal for Arcelor Mittal to launch a $1-billion iron ore mining project that will eventually employ 20,000 and is expected to begin exports next year after the company refurbishes train tracks damaged during the West African country's long civil conflict. In Senegal, a joint public-private Indian group has invested $250 million in exchange for a stake in the colonial-era enterprise, Industries Chimiques du Senegal, with rock phosphate mines and plants to produce phosphoric acid used in agriculture. On a more modest level, in April 2010, the Indian investment company JSW paid about $12 million to obtain a majority stake in South African Coal Mining Holdings, a coal producer started by the traditional monarchy of the Bafokeng people to exploit the resources on their tribal lands in the North West Province.[34]

Indian firms are also beginning to see in Africa a possible solution to their country's food security challenge as formerly agricultural lands are lost to urbanization and industrialization. A few years ago, for example, two Indian firms, Ms Mashuli Gashmani Ltd. and Angelique, invested a total of $12 million in Uganda to establish, respectively, a commercial prawn fishery and turnkey aquaculture development. Uganda has become something of a favorite for Indian agricultural investment. At the end of 2009, Jay Shree Tea & Industries—a part of the B.K. Birla group of companies that has extensive tea-growing holdings in Assam, Darjeeling, Jalpaiguri, Uttar Dinajpur, and Tamil Nadu—announced plans for its first overseas acquisition in Uganda as well as plans to establish itself in Kenya.[35] Such enterprises will undoubtedly proliferate as India, where the average food energy intake per person is still below 2500 kcal and the population is set to grow at an average of over 1 percent per year over the next 3 decades, overtakes China as the major driver of growth in world demand for agricultural products.[36] In fact, individual Indian states like Punjab have begun exploring possible accords with African countries for the export of agricultural technology and investment in exchange for access to land for rice cultivation.[37]

Opportunities for Indian Businesses.

India's nonoil bilateral trade with Africa has grown in just 1 decade from $4.8 billion in 1998 to $34.5 billion in 2008.[38] One report published by Chatham House (formerly the Royal Institute of International Affairs), noting that African countries are proving to be very attractive to Indian investors, observes that "India has sought to gain a foothold in these countries by writing off debts owed under the Heavily Indebted Poor Countries [HIPC] Initiative and restructuring commercial debts. At the same time, the Export-Import (EXIM) Bank has extended lines of credit to governments, commercial banks, financial institutions, and regional development banks."[39] India has cancelled the debts of five HIPCs in Africa—Ghana, Mozambique, Tanzania, Uganda, and Zambia—while its EXIM Bank has extended lines of credit to institutions in a number of African countries, including Angola, Djibouti, Ghana, South Africa, Sudan, Togo, and Zambia.

Since the launch of the Indian Technical and Economic Cooperation (ITEC) program in 1964, New Delhi has leveraged its human capital strengths to forge ties with developing countries, providing assistance to some 154 states since then.[40] In fact, some 60 percent of the training slots in the ITEC program have historically been reserved for Africans.[41] As a farewell tribute to outgoing president A. P. J. Abdul Kalam as he left office in July 2007, the Indian cabinet approved an initial $100 million for the Pan-African E-Network he proposed to bridge the digital divide on the continent through a network of satellite, fiber optics, and wireless connections that would also highlight India's strengths in the technological and medical sectors. As a first phase of the initiative, seven universities and 12 advanced hospitals in India are to be linked to five universities, 53 clinics, and 53 distance education centers in Africa.[42] Of course, this type of scientific and technical cooperation, over time, can mature into economic ties. Within the framework of the Techno-Economic Approach for Africa-India Movement (TEAM-9) it launched in 2004, India has extended over $500 million credit on highly favorable terms to eight African countries (Burkina Faso, Chad, Côte d'Ivoire, Equatorial Guinea, Ghana, Guinea-Bissau, Mali, and Senegal) linked to the purchase of Indian goods and services; a number of other African countries have lined up to join the program. Cumulatively, these initiatives highlight the increasing maturity of the effort to integrate India's commercial and political diplomacy.[43]

Major private sector Indian industrial conglomerates like the Tata Group and the Mahindra Group have made considerable headway in Africa — the former's Nano automobile, considered the world's cheapest car at $2,500, as well as its more upscale Aria, priced at approximately $15,000, have been especially attractive for the cohort of Africans just joining the middle class[44] — as have infrastructure-building concerns like KEC International, the overseas arm of Kamani Engineering Corporation, which has projects in Algeria, Ethiopia, Ghana, Kenya, Libya, Mozambique, South Africa, Tunisia, and Zambia. Government-owned concerns are also profiting from large-scale projects, especially where official Indian development assistance is involved. For example, Senegal used a grant from the Indian Ministry of External Affairs to hire the RITES consultancy owned by the Indian Ministry of Railways to conduct a feasibility study of constructing a railroad linking the Dakar-Tambacounda line with Ziguinchor in the economically disadvantaged Casamance region. RITES has also had consulting contracts in Kenya and Mozambique and been involved in road design work in Ethiopia and Uganda. Another enterprise owned by the Ministry of Railways, Ircon International, has built railways in Algeria, Mozambique, Nigeria, Sudan, and Zambia.

Leading exports from India to Africa currently include machinery, transport equipment, paper and other wood products, textiles, plastics, and chemical and pharmaceutical products. With HIV/AIDS and other diseases ravaging the continent and driving up demand for lower-cost generic anti-retrovirals and other drugs, Indian pharmaceutical firms like Cipla and Ranbaxy have opened entirely new markets. According to the Confederation of Indian Industry (CII), trade between the subcontinent and Africa has been growing at the annual rate of 25 percent in recent years. In October 2006, a CII-sponsored "Conclave on India-Africa Project Partnership" in New Delhi attracted over 750 delegates and produced business deals worth $17 billion.[45] The CII subsequently followed up in the summer of 2007 with a series of "regional conclaves" held in Kampala, Uganda, Maputo, Mozambique, and Abidjan, Côte d'Ivoire, which drew representatives of the public and private sectors from a total of 42 African countries to meet with their counterparts from India. The Sixth CII-EXIM India-Africa Project Partnership Conference in New Delhi in March 2010 brought together government ministers, business executives, and experts who discussed some 145 projects worth $9 billion.[46] These encounters have not been without impressive results: in Ethiopia alone, about 500 Indian companies had invested more than $5 billion by the end of 2009.[47]

Indian firms have also become increasingly visible with their interest and investment in the telecommunications sector in Africa. In early 2010, the Indian steel group Essar, itself a minority shareholder in Vodafone's operations in India, announced plans to invest $2 billion in six or seven African mobile businesses.[48] Meanwhile, India's largest telecommunications services provider, Bharti Airtel, concluded a record-breaking $10.7-billion-dollar deal to take over the Kuwait-based Zain Group's mobile operations in

15 African countries, making it the largest telecom provider in Africa and the fifth largest in the world.[49] While vastly different in many respects, India and Africa are very similar in others, especially in those areas relevant to developing the telecommunications sector. In both the subcontinent and the continent, mobile telephony has been the means through which hundreds of millions have gained their first access to telecommunications services for voice communication and messaging. The economic and social impact of this development — the result of both technological advances and market liberalizations — are just beginning to be felt. The transfer of technologies and experience from Indian operators will undoubtedly accelerate Africa's progress. As Indian Commerce Minister Anand Sharma noted during the India-Africa Project Partnership summit in early 2010:

> India's engagement with Africa is distinct and different from any other country. It's a partnership, a friendship which is rooted well in history. We are not in competition. . . . Africa appreciates India's multi-sectoral engagement and also its abiding commitment to capacity-building of human resource and in building institutions in Africa.[50]

Diplomatic In-Roads.

Over the last decade, the India foreign policy establishment has endeavored to overcome the institutional neglect to which it was constrained to consign Africa after the promising start of the immediate post-independence period. Until 2003, the Ministry of External Affairs had only one joint secretary with responsibility for the singular Africa division; today, three joint secretaries manage three regional divisions covering the continent. During the last decade of the

20th century, India was closing down diplomatic missions in Africa as an economy measure; in contrast, at the end of the first decade of the 21st century, New Delhi maintained 26 embassies or high commissions on the continent in addition to honorary consuls-general in 15 countries where there is no resident ambassador or high commissioner.[51] A multilateral India-Africa summit consciously modeled on the historic October 2006 Beijing summit of the Forum on China-Africa Cooperation (FOCAC), which brought nearly 50 African heads of state and ministers to the Chinese capital, the Africa-India Forum was held in New Delhi in April 2008 leading to the adoption of a "Joint Declaration of the Africa-India Partnership," as well as its articulation of an "Africa-India Framework for Cooperation."[52] The Indian government subsequently allocated $6 billion to implement the promises of the cooperation forum.[53] Such diplomatic attention has already paid off. In 2006, for example, the chair of the Council of Ministers of the Economic Community of West African States (ECOWAS), Foreign Minister Aïchatou Mindaoudou of Niger, threw the weight of the 15-member subregional group behind India's bid for a seat on the United Nations Security Council (UNSC). More recently, in a lecture he delivered on Africa Day in May 2010, Indian External Affairs Minister Pranab Mukherjee linked the country's bid for a permanent seat on the UNSC with Africa's own candidacy:

> The current global architecture is many decades old and is no longer capable of adequately meeting the increasing challenges before us. The United Nations, in particular, needs to be reformed and strengthened. The absence of Africa and countries like India from the permanent membership of the UN Security Council makes the body unrepresentative and undemocratic.

India strongly supports Africa's demand to get its due role as permanent members of the Security Council. We appreciate the widespread support of African countries for India's permanent membership of the Security Council.[54]

However, unlike their Chinese counterparts, who have made travels through Africa an almost seasonal ritual, India leaders have been strangely reluctant to visit the continent despite its growing importance. Before Prime Minister Manmohan Singh's October 2007 visit to Abuja, the last time an Indian head of government had paid a visit to Nigeria, India's second largest source of oil, was 1962! Fortunately, this pattern is quickly changing. Three months before the prime minister's visit to Nigeria (from which country he continued onward to South Africa), External Affairs Minister Mukherjee visited Ethiopia not only to meet with then-African Union Commission Chairperson Alpha Oumar Konaré, but also to sign a series of wide-ranging bilateral economic and political agreements with his Ethiopian hosts. During his sojourn in the Ethiopian capital, Mukherjee convened a conference of the heads of India's diplomatic missions in Africa to announce a more active policy toward the continent.

On a more ambitious global level, a loose political alliance of India, Brazil, and South Africa, formally called the India-Brazil-South Africa (IBSA) Dialogue Forum, was launched in 2004 with the goal of achieving common positions at the UN, the Doha Rounds, and other multilateral settings for the three major "southern" nations.[55] Annual summits of the leaders of the IBSA states have so far been held in Brasilia (2006), Pretoria (2007), New Delhi (2008), and Brasilia (2010). The cornerstone of this grouping is clearly the important historical links between India and the ruling African National Congress. At the end of talks in July 2007 between the foreign ministers of the three countries, the nations agreed to strengthen their mutual ties by increasing their trade 50 percent by 2010 from its current level of $10 billion. Commerce between India and South Africa is expected to account for most of the boost.[56]

If India's diplomatic action in Africa has been, until recently, relatively modest, that is not to say that the reach of its "soft power" has not been impressive. In addition to the tremendous amount of good will that New Delhi has banked from the constant support given to African liberation movements at both the bilateral and multilateral levels in the second half of the 20th century, there are the large numbers of African students who are trained in Indian universities and technical institutes each year. Due to a combination of quality instruction, lower fees and other costs (when scholarships do not cover all expenses), and relatively easier entry requirements, more than 10,000 African students enroll each year in Indian institutions.[57] In addition, India's Ministry of Science and Technology has launched a program that will offer 416 fellowships to African scientists — eight from each country — to conduct research in various fields ranging from biotechnology to forestry at top Indian institutions, including the prestigious Indian Institutes of Technology, the All India Institute of Medical Sciences, and the National Institute of Ocean Technology. Tellingly, the government designated the Federation of Indian Chambers of Commerce and Industry (FICCI) as the coordinator for the new program.[58] In time, most of these scholars will return to their home countries to assume positions of responsibility from which many will promote good relations with India.

An Emerging Power's Military Engagements.

The shadow of the nonviolent Mahatma Gandhi notwithstanding, India's leadership has recognized that a rising power also needs the ability to project "hard power" in proportion to its economic and other elements of its "soft power."[59] India today has the world's third largest army, fourth-largest air force, and seventh-largest navy.[60]

Although New Delhi has played an active role in UN peacekeeping operations since the first mission to the former Belgian Congo in 1960, it has been particularly since the end of the Cold War that, as befits a responsible stakeholder in the international system, India has put its military at the service of global order, participating in numerous UN peacekeeping operations, many in Africa. Among other deployments, Indian forces have been involved in "blue helmet" missions in Mozambique, Somalia, Angola, Sierra Leone, Ethiopia, Eritrea, the Democratic Republic of the Congo (DRC), and Liberia. The Indian contingent serving in the DRC represents the largest national contribution to the recently renamed UN Organization Stabilization Mission in the Democratic Republic of the Congo (MONUSCO), while the contingent that originally deployed in January 2007 to the UN Mission in Liberia (UNMIL) under Commander Seema Dhundia enjoys the distinction of being the first (and still only) all-female UN peacekeeping unit ever deployed in international peacekeeping. The then-special representative of the UN Secretary-General hailed the deployment of the unit from India's Central Reserve Police Force as "a new beginning for gender equality in peacekeeping" and expressed the hope that its presence would be "an encouragement for Liberian women to come forward and help rebuild their country by participating in the forces of law and order."[61] See Table 1 for UN peacekeeping missions in Africa that included Indian participation.

Operation	Country	Duration
United Nations Operation in the Congo (ONUC)	Congo	1960-1964
United Nations Angola Verification Mission I (UNAVEM I)	Angola	1989
United Nations Transition Assistance Group (UNTAG)	Namibia	1989-1990
United Nations Angola Verification Mission II (UNAVEM II)	Angola	1991-1995
United Nations Operation in Somalia II (UNOSOM II)	Somalia	1993-1995
United Nations Operation in Mozambique (ONUMOZ)	Mozambique	1992-1994
United Nations Observer Mission in Liberia (UNOMIL)	Liberia	1993-1997
United Nations Assistance Mission for Rwanda (UNAMIR)	Rwanda	1993-1996
United Nations Angola Verification Mission III (UNAVEM III)	Angola	1995-1997
United Nations Observer Mission in Sierra Leone (UNOMSIL)	Sierra Leone	1998-1999
United Nations Observer Mission in Angola (MONUA)	Angola	1997-1999
United Nations Mission in Sierra Leone (UNAMSIL)	Sierra Leone	1999-2005
United Nations Mission in Ethiopia and Eritrea (UNMEE)	Ethiopia, Eritrea	2000-2008
United Nations Organization Mission in the DRC (MONUC)/ United Nations Stabilization Mission in the DRC (MONUSCO)	DRC	1999-?
United Nations Mission in Liberia (UNMIL)	Liberia	2003-?
United Nations Operation in Burundi (ONUB)	Burundi	2004-?
United Nations Operation in Côte d'Ivoire (ONUCI)	Côte d'Ivoire	2004-?
United Nations Mission in Sudan (UNMIS)	Sudan	2005-?

Sources: Ian Cardozo, ed., *The Indian Army: Brief History*, New Delhi, India: United Services Institution of India, 2005; United Nations Peacekeeping, "Current Operations" and "Past Operations," available at *www.un.org/en/peacekeeping/*.

Table 1. UN Peacekeeping Missions in Africa in Which India Has Participated.

Overall, India is the third-largest contributor of manpower to UN peacekeeping, its 8,759 military and police personnel being just slightly less than the numbers deployed by its neighbors on the subcontinent, Pakistan and Bangladesh.[62] Even more significantly, the overwhelming majority of Indian peacekeepers were, as of mid-2010, deployed to operations in Africa, with approximately 7,500 personnel in the blue-helmeted missions in Côte d'Ivoire, the DRC, Liberia, and Sudan, [63] thus dwarfing the combined contributions of all five permanent members of the UNSC in Africa.[64] Indians also occupy senior positions within these missions, including the Force Commander of the operation in the DRC, Lieutenant General Chander Prakash; the Deputy Special Representative of the UN Secretary-General in Sudan, Jasber Singh Lidder; and the Police Commissioner of the Liberia mission, Gautam Sawang. See Table 2 for the current top contributors to African UN peacekeeping missions.

UN Mission	Pakistan	Bangladesh	India	Nigeria	Egypt
MINURSO	11	9	0	7	24
MONUC/	3,646	2,819	4,600	23	1,025
MONUSCO UNMIL	2,938	1,471	248	1,718	15
ONUCI	1,275	2,346	8	5	180
UNMIS	1,522	1,656	2,701	48	1,539
UNAMID	788	1,349	0	3,705	2,616
MINURCAT	6	151	0	4	10
Total	10,186	9,801	7,549	5,510	5,409

Source: United Nations Peacekeeping, UN Missions Summary Detailed by Country, June 30, 2010; available at *www.un.org/en/ peacekeeping/contributors/2010/june10_3.pd.*

**Table 2. Current Top Contributors
to the UN Peacekeeping Missions in Africa.**

In addition, drawing on its own long experience, India has also helped train the South African National Defense Force (SANDF) for peacekeeping missions now that the end of apartheid has made it possible for South Africa to do its part in regional security efforts.[65] While not all of these Indian deployments to Africa have been stunning successes—the contretemps of Major-General Vijay Jetley's tenure as commander of the UN Mission in Sierra Leone (UNAMSIL) are legendary in the annals of peacekeeping[66]—they nonetheless represent an extraordinary commitment to collective security burden-sharing, despite not-insignificant domestic and international constraints. Of course, from the point of view of its own national interests, India's track record with UN peacekeeping operations has its own strategic, operational, and tactical value. Moreover, it allows the Indian defense staff, even in times of economic belt-tightening, to make the case for continued investment in the reach capabilities of its air force and navy.[67] See Table 3 for India's current UN Peacekeeping Mission contributions.

	Troops	Police	Military Observers and Other Experts	Total
MONUC/ MONUSCO	4,257	250	48	4,555
UNMIL	0	244	4	248
ONUCI	0	25	0	25
UNMIS	2,637	46	18	2,701
Total	6,894	565	70	7,529

Source: United Nations Peacekeeping, UN Missions Summary Detailed by Country, June 30, 2009, available at *www.un.org/en/ peacekeeping/contributors/2010/june10_3.pdf.*

Table 3. India's Current Contribution to UN Peacekeeping Missions in Africa.

As part of its defense diplomacy, India has also invested in future African military leaders, over the years training thousands of officers from a number of African countries in the academies of its three service branches, as well as the postgraduate National Defence College in New Delhi and Defence Services Staff College in Wellington. Among the beneficiaries of this type of advanced training was Nigeria's Olusegun Obasanjo who, in turn, during both his tenures in the presidency (military ruler, 1976-79; civilian president, 1999-2007) hosted Indian military chiefs of staff for talks aimed at strengthening defense cooperation. As a result of these ties, India was involved in the transformation of the Nigerian Defence Academy in Kaduna into the tertiary-level degree-granting Nigerian Military University.

In February and March 2007, Vice-Admiral J. Mudimu, chief of the South African Navy, paid an extended visit to his Indian counterpart, Admiral Sureesh

Mehta, chief of the Naval Staff of the Indian Navy, to work out the mechanisms for cooperation between the two countries for regional security in the Indian Ocean, particularly for dealing with terrorism and piracy. The two officers also explored the possibility of creating a naval component of the IBSA alliance and discussed the first IBSA Joint Naval Exercises (IBSA-MAR), held off the Cape coast of South Africa in May 2008, which was aimed at establishing commonalities of tactical approaches and aim for procedural interoperability of their forces.

Whatever becomes of this South-South military cooperation exercise, it remains that the Indian navy is a particularly important part of its engagement in the Indian Ocean and a vital force of stability in the region—as evidenced by its ability to quickly deploy after the tsunami at the end of 2004, when it joined Australia, Japan, and the United States to form the "core group" that coordinated the initial international response. As the threat of piracy continues to rise in the western Indian Ocean off the coast of Somalia, it is likely that India will play an increasing role in ensuring the safety of the sea lanes, especially since the naval resources of the United States and the European Union are stretched by other operations, even as senior naval officers of these countries publicly express reluctance to continue supporting the extended deployments of their task forces in the region.[68] In fact, after several of its merchant vessels were attacked by Somali pirates, India was one of the first countries to send naval forces against the marauders, and in November 2008, the *Talwar*-class frigate INS *Tabar* engaged and sank a Thai trawler with links to international organized crime that had been used as a pirate "mother ship" on various occasions.[69]

With the entire Indian Ocean regarded by the country's strategic elite as falling within its security perimeter,[70] it is not surprising that India should be forging stronger ties with states along the East African littoral — signing defense agreements with Kenya, Madagascar, and Mozambique and initiating naval joint training programs with Kenya, Mozambique, South Africa, and Tanzania. The Indian Navy has even been extending its maritime security cover to most of the islands off that subregion. Since 2003, when a bilateral defense assistance accord was signed, the Indian Navy has patrolled the Exclusive Economic Zone (EEZ) of Mauritius. A similar deal has led to patrols of the territorial waters of the Seychelles. In June and July 2003, the *Rajput*-class destroyer INS *Ranjit* and the *Sukyana*-class patrol boat INS *Suvarna* were deployed off Maputo at the invitation of the Mozambican government to help provide security for the African Union summit taking place there. In June 2004, two other *Sukyana*-class patrol boats, INS *Sujata* and INS *Savitri*, assisted with security for the World Economic Forum taking place in Mozambique. This cooperation led the two countries to eventually sign a memorandum of understanding in March 2006, whereby India agreed to mount regular maritime patrols off the Mozambican coast.[71] In 2007, India established its first listening post on foreign soil in northern Madagascar, setting up a radar surveillance station with sophisticated digital systems to track shipping in the western Indian Ocean.[72] There have also been repeated rumors in the subregion of India's interest in leasing the remote Agalega Islands from Mauritius, ostensibly for tourist development, but possibly for a naval base.[73]

The relatively small Indian defense industrial sector has also made some forays recently into Africa, supplying patrol vessels (SDB Mk-2 seaward defense boats) and light helicopters (SA-316B *Alouette III* and SA-315B *Lama* craft) to several African states.[74] India has also become a major customer for South Africa's arms exports according to one assessment by the U.S. intelligence community.[75] Relations between the South African arms industry and the India Ministry of Defense have been close.

The Impact on Africa.

While the growing influence of any other major non-African actor on the continent bears very careful watching, there are a number of reasons why New Delhi's increased engagement in Africa, unlike that of some others, ought to be cautiously welcomed by Africans. First, there is no doubt that Africa stands to benefit from the addition of India to the list of countries seeking access to the continent's natural resources and markets as well as political and strategic partnerships with African states. This is especially true if African leaders are able to develop a strategic approach that leverages their strengthened bargaining position. In recent years, for example, it was revealed that India pays the highest prices for South African spot coal.[76]

Second, in general it could be said that India's *modus operandi* on the continent not only benefits Indians; it also benefits Africans. As Karen Monaghan, then National Intelligence Fellow at the Council on Foreign Relations, has observed, India can teach Africa a few things about the "importance of entrepreneurship" for "driving and generating jobs, and generating income, and generating growth." She notes that "Indian companies are much more integrated into African society and the African economy," hiring locally and emphasizing training Africans on how to maintain and repair the plants they build.[77] Unlike China, which is often viewed, not without some justification, as a predator interested only in extracting commodities, India has encouraged technology transfers to its African partners,[78] gearing its projects in Africa, according to one former secretary in the Ministry of External Affairs, toward "creating value-addition for its natural resources, generating local employment, transfer of technology, and developing its human resources."[79] Kenyan entrepreneur James Shikwati has argued that "unlike China that focuses mostly on trade and aid, India is focusing on empowerment and infrastructure development . . . on having its companies get more integrated into African society by hiring locally, training Africans, and increasing the stakes of Africans in Indian businesses."[80]

Third, Africa must profit from the lessons that India learned with the economic liberalization begun in the 1990s under then-Finance Minister Manmohan Singh, thus freeing itself from the stultifying 3.5-percent annual rate of economic growth that just barely kept pace with the population increase.[81] These lessons are precisely those that African states need to study for their own development, rather than harkening to the "no strings attached" blandishments that are offered to them by China's mercantilist mandarins. Moreover, for African states, many of which are plagued by instability, autocracy, and ethnic and religious strife, India offers the example of a successfully developing country where speakers of 22 different official languages (in addition to English) as well as an estimated 1,652 mother tongues have coexisted largely peacefully for 6 decades. Despite such astonishing linguistic diversity, India has acquired ever-greater national consciousness while building the world's largest democracy. Despite its difficult birth as an independent nation in the midst of the religious partition that created Pakistan, India is home to what, by most measures, is the second largest Muslim population of any nation in the world. Indeed, from 2002 until 2007, the president of India, Abdul Kalam, was a Muslim. The current prime minister, Manmohan Singh, is, as his name indicates, a Sikh, while the chair of the governing Congress Party-led coalition, Sonia Gandhi, *née* Sonia Antonia Maino, is the Italian-born Roman Catholic widow of assassinated former prime minister Rajiv Gandhi, a Hindu. As Prime Minister Singh has noted:

> If there is an "idea of India" by which India should be defined, it is the idea of an inclusive, open, multi-cultural, multi-ethnic, multi-lingual society. I believe that this is the dominant trend of political evolution of all societies in the 21st century. Therefore, we have an obligation to history and mankind to show that pluralism works. India must show that democracy can deliver development and empower the marginalized. Liberal democracy is the natural order of political organization in today's world. All alternate systems, authoritarian and majoritarian in varying degrees, are an aberration.[82]

Africans have not failed to pick up on this. For example, Greg Mills, head of the Johannesburg-based Brenthurst Foundation, a think tank devoted to strengthening economic performance in Africa, has argued:

> This is the India which has allowed 100 percent foreign ownership where previously it was forbidden, the free repatriation of profits and capital investment, tax holidays for infrastructure projects, the lifting of

31

controls in capital markets, and the slashing of import tariffs. That and its democratic dividend are especially what the India of today can lend and teach the Africa of tomorrow.[83]

Fourth, the burgeoning Indian-African relationship presents good prospects for security and stability in Africa. India has enormous political capital from its co-founding and longtime leadership of the Non-Aligned Movement, as well as its support of anti-colonial and anti-apartheid movements on the African continent. On the other hand, no country has lost more of its citizens to Islamist violence than India which, even today, remains one of the states most targeted by *jihadis* and thus has a direct stake in countering terrorism and defeating (or at least pacifying) radical Islamism, which threatens the peace across a wide swath of Africa. India's history enables its government to articulate the anti-extremism, pro-democracy message credibly in places where, quite simply, the credibility of the United States and other Western nations is very limited.

Implications for the United States and Its Strategy in Africa.

The 2006 *National Security Strategy of the United States of America*, issued by the administration of President George W. Bush, declared that "Africa holds growing geo-strategic importance and is a high priority of this administration"[84] — as well it should for a region that not only currently supplies the United States with more hydrocarbons than the Middle East, but also presents significant political, security, and humanitarian challenges. However, although America may well still be the most powerful external actor on the African continent, it is certainly no longer unchallenged. As the most recent iteration of the *National Security Strategy*, released by the administration of President Obama in May 2010 acknowledged, "China and India—the world's two most populous nations—are becoming more engaged globally."[85] And perhaps nowhere is this better illustrated than on the African continent where "these countries, along with traditional Western powers, are increasingly turning to Africa to meet their energy and other resource needs"[86] to sustain their economic growth. Moreover, "the shift to a strategic view of Africa underscores the continent's growing importance in the structures of global governance and the imperative for external powers to secure Africa's support in advancing the global agenda on terms that better serve their national interests."[87]

In this view, the burgeoning Indian-African relationship is good for the United States overall, especially given the strategic partnership that America and India have forged in recent years.[88] Not only is India "an answer to some of our major geopolitical problems,"[89] but as former U.S. Ambassador to India Robert Blackwill has put it, the United States can benefit in many of its security preoccupations in Africa from the tacit—and occasionally explicit—support of India. As former Secretary of State Henry Kissinger has pointed out, in an age of terrorism and potential "clash of civilizations," both India and the United States pursue parallel objectives with respect to radical Islamism.[90] Hence, New Delhi potentially represents an ideal partner for advancing a positive agenda to counter extremism and terrorism in Africa. Secretary of State Hillary Rodham Clinton recently affirmed: "Both India and the United States have seen our cities and our citizens targeted by violent extremists, and we share concerns about the continuing threat of terrorism, and we share concerns about the dangers of nuclear proliferation. For our peoples, security is more than a priority; it is an imperative."[91]

Of course, policymakers in the United States would be mistaken to expect a proud and democratic nation like India to serve simply as its messenger boy, much less its lackey. As one scholar told a congressional hearing, the country's large size, ancient history, and great ambitions ensure that "India will likely march to the beat of its own drummer."[92] Nevertheless, with respect to India's enlarging profile in Africa, political and other opinion leaders must not give rein to the alarmism that has characterized their policy discussions about the PRC's political and commercial investments in the continent. India is not likely to present a direct challenge to the core interests of the United States and its allies in what is now recognized to be the geostrategically vital region of Sub-Saharan Africa.[93] In fact, as it plays commercial catch-up (India's exports amount to just 10 percent of China's), the subcontinental country's economic interests are more likely than not to clash with those of the Middle Kingdom[94] — a development that might be greeted by some with undiplomatic enthusiasm, given the serious challenge that China's expansion in Africa has posed.[95] As one analyst has noted, the U.S.-Indian relationship "should not be judged in terms of immediate deliverables, but the gradual convergence of national interests."[96] And many of India's national interests, like maintaining peace and security along the Indian Ocean littoral, including the eastern coast of Africa, align quite well with America's broader military and strategic interests in the same area.[97]

From an American perspective, what steps might therefore be taken to enhance the U.S.-Indian relationship overall and foster cooperation in Africa that advances both countries' interests? First, U.S. leaders need to reaffirm explicitly the commitment made under President George W. Bush to "help make India a major world power in the twenty-first century."[98] The articulation of this goal helped achieve a strategic breakthrough in U.S.-India relations, overcoming chasms of Cold War-era political and nonproliferation disagreements. In general, the new foundations laid for U.S. ties with India beginning with President Bill Clinton are still fresh enough to not have entirely settled. Hence "there is a need for a more proactive policy towards India that helps secure its national objectives and, in so doing, makes it easier to attain broader U.S. goals."[99] While the development of a strong India is a long-term objective, U.S. policymakers and analysts need to be more aware in the short term that the achievement of that goal is closely linked to India's current efforts to secure access to African resources, markets, and partners. Moreover, in pursuit of these, India plays a constructive role in both ensuring stability as well as promoting the democratic values it shares with the United States.

Second, especially in Africa, U.S. interests are more than partially served by India's involvement in bilateral and multilateral security initiatives with its African partners. The willingness of New Delhi to commit to peacekeeping, peace enforcement, and nation-building efforts — that Washington has largely lacked either the political will or the resources to engage in — on the African continent has complemented other American activities aimed at promoting greater stability. The readiness of the Indian Navy to help create a maritime security framework in the western Indian Ocean is also a valuable contribution. Hence, cooperation between the U.S. and Indian security engagements in Africa is highly desirable. Opportunities for regular exchanges between the regional military forces of the two countries ought to be increased at all levels. While the Indian military is eager to gain access to U.S. technology and other capabilities, U.S. forces would also benefit from the operational experience of their Indian counterparts in Africa as well as the entrée that they enjoy in many countries. The permanent hosting of an Indian liaison officer at AFRICOM headquarters in Stuttgart, Germany, and at the Combined Joint Task Force-Horn of Africa (CJTF-HOA) in Djibouti would be an important step forward. The leadership of U.S. Naval Forces Africa (NAVAF) and U.S. Naval Forces Central Command (NAVCENT) should develop ways to partner with their Indian Navy counterparts to implement the Indo-U.S. Framework for Maritime Security Cooperation signed in 2006 by President Bush and Prime Minister Singh.[100] The Framework committed the two countries to work together to address piracy and armed robbery at sea, as well as to conduct bilateral maritime exercises, cooperate in search and rescue at sea, and exchange information.

In short, while one should not gloss over potential differences or overstate what is achievable in the short term, there is nonetheless a significant set of complementary interests that both sides would find beneficial to secure.

Conclusion.

India has clearly demonstrated not only that it has extensive interests in Africa, but that it is willing to invest significant amounts of human, political, and material capital in order to advance those interests. While India's ties with Africa in the modern era predate its independence, in recent years the nature of the engagement has changed through the expansion of the country's commercial and economic relations with Africa and its growing cooperation in the energy sector. New Delhi's geopolitical ambitions have likewise been a motivating factor in its involvement in Africa, especially its support for UN peacekeeping efforts and its expansion of its maritime security cover to the archipelagic and littoral nations of East Africa.

By and large, the goals of Indian engagements in Africa and the means by which it has pursued them are not opposed to the strategic objectives sought by U.S. policy as laid out in the current *National Security Strategy* document:

> Our economic, security, and political cooperation will be consultative and encompass global, regional, and national priorities including access to open markets, conflict prevention, global peacekeeping, counterterrorism, and the protection of vital carbon sinks. The Administration will refocus its priorities on strategic interventions that can promote job creation and economic growth; combat corruption while strengthening good governance and accountability; responsibly improve the capacity of African security and rule of law sectors; and work through diplomatic dialogue to mitigate local and regional tensions before they become crises. . . .
>
> When international forces are needed to respond to threats and keep the peace, we will work with international partners to ensure they are ready, able, and willing. We will continue to build support in other countries to contribute to sustaining global peace and

stability operations, through U.N. peacekeeping and regional organizations, such as NATO and the African Union. We will continue to broaden the pool of troop and police contributors, working to ensure that they are properly trained and equipped, that their mandates are matched to means, and that their missions are backed by the political action necessary to build and sustain peace.[101]

This being America's foreign policy toward Africa, then, insofar as its mission is to conduct "sustained security engagement through military-to-military programs, military-sponsored activities, and other military operations as directed to promote a stable and secure African environment in support of U.S. foreign policy,"[102] AFRICOM needs to develop greater awareness of India's activities on the continent, and also the appropriate mechanisms with which to engage and, as appropriate, to partner with Indian forces serving with UN peacekeeping missions and other Indian initiatives in Africa, especially those aimed at building the capacities of African governments and institutions. This would entail not only lending support where called upon, but also learning from the rather extensive experience of the Indian military in Africa. The scope for activities—from officer exchanges to senior visits, seminars and subject-matter expert exchanges to technical cooperation and joint exercises—is vast. In turn, this military-led cooperation in one specific theater can support the overall fundamental shift in bilateral relations that has been indicated by the highest civilian authority. Other parts of the interagency should undertake similar efforts, for example, allowing Indian diplomatic assets to take the lead in multilateral forums where the interests of the two countries are complementary and India's voice may find greater resonance with the intended audience.

President Obama has described India as a "rising and responsible global power," adding that "the relationship between the United States and India will be one of the defining partnerships of the twenty-first century."[103] A former U.S. ambassador to India has gone even further, arguing that:

> It is safe to say that the alignment between India and the United States is now an enduring part of the international landscape of the 21st century. The vital interests of both Washington and New Delhi are now so congruent that the two countries can and will find many ways in which to cooperate in the decades ahead. Over time, the U.S.-India relationship will come more and more to resemble the intimate U.S. interaction with Japan and our European treaty allies.[104]

This type of strategic partnership, however, requires constant nurturing across multiple arenas. It cannot be taken for granted. Even though both an American president and an Indian prime minister have noted in recent years that the two countries are "natural partners," it is essential that we continue to nurture our underlying affinities with vigilance, energy, and understanding.

ENDNOTES

1. Barack Obama, Remarks to the Ghanaian Parliament, Accra, Ghana, July 11, 2009, available from *www.whitehouse.gov/the_press_office/Remarks-by-the-President-to-the-Ghanaian-Parliament*.

2. *Ibid.*

3. *Ibid.*

4. U.S. Africa Command, Fact Sheet, "United States Africa Command," October 18, 2008, available from *www.africom.mil/getArticle.asp?art=1644*.

5. Manmohan Singh, Statement at the Fifteenth Summit of the Non-Aligned Movement, Sharm-el-Sheikh, Egypt, July 15, 2009, available from *www.pmindia.nic.in/visits/content.asp?id=270*.

6. See *inter alia*, Garth le Pere and Garth Shelton, "Afro-Chinese Relations: An Evolving South-South Partnership," *South African Journal of International Affairs*, Vol. 13, No. 1, Summer/Autumn 2006, pp. 33-55; J. Peter Pham, "China's African Strategy and Its Implications for U.S. Interests," *American Foreign Policy Interests*, Vol. 28, No. 3, May/June 2006, pp. 239-253; Dennis M. Tull, "China's Engagement in Africa: Scope, Significance and Consequences," *Journal of Modern African Studies*, Vol. 44, No. 3, September 2006, pp. 459-479; Chris Alden, *China in Africa*, London: Zed Books, 2007; Serge Michel and Michel Beuret with Paolo Woods, *La Chinafrique: Pékin à la conquête du continent noir* (*Chinafrica: Beijing Conquers the Dark Continent*), Paris, France: Bernard Grasset, 2008; and Sarah Raine, *China's African Challenges*, London, UK: International Institute for Strategic Studies, 2009.

7. See *inter alia*, Donovan C. Chau, *Political Warfare in Sub-Saharan Africa: U.S. Capabilities and Chinese Operations in Ethiopia, Kenya, Nigeria, and South Africa*, Carlisle, PA: Strategic Studies Institute, U.S. Army War College, 2007; Philippe D. Rogers, "China and United Nations Peacekeeping Operations in Africa," *Naval War College Review*, Vol. 60, No. 2, Spring 2007, pp. 73-93; and Richard Weitz, "Operation Somalia: China's First Expeditionary Force," *China Security*, Vol. 5, No. 1, Winter 2009, pp. 27-43.

8. See *inter alia*, François Lafargue, "L'Inde: Une puissance africaine" ("India: An African Power"), *Défense nationale et sécurité collective*, Vol. 63, No. 1, January 2007, pp. 111-117; J. Peter Pham, "India's Expanding Relations with Africa and Their Implications for U.S. Interests," *American Foreign Policy Interests*, Vol. 29, No. 5, September/October 2007, pp. 341-352; Sanusha Naidu, "India's Growing African Strategy," *Review of African Political Economy*, Vol. 35, No. 115, March 2008, pp. 116-128.

9. See R. Nicholas Burns, "America's Strategic Opportunity with India: The New U.S.-India Partnership," *Foreign Affairs*, Vol. 86, No. 6, November/December 2007, pp. 131-146; also see Teresita C. Schaffer, *India and the United States in the 21st Century: Reinventing Partnership*, Washington, DC: Center for Strategic and International Studies, 2009.

10. C. Raja Mohan, "India and the Balance of Power," *Foreign Affairs*, Vol. 85, No. 4, July/August 2006, pp. 17-18.

11. Basil Davidson, *Africa in History: Themes and Outlines*, Rev. Ed., New York: Touchstone, 1995, p. 78.

12. See Robert G. Gregory, *India and East Africa: A History of Race Relations within the British Empire, 1890-1939*, Oxford, UK: Clarendon Press, 1971.

13. See Ali A. Mazrui, *Africa's International Relations: The Diplomacy of Dependency and Change*, Boulder, CO: Lynne Rienner, 1977, pp. 117-118.

14. Quoted in T. G. Ramamurthi, "Foundations of India's Africa Policy," *Africa Quarterly*, Vol. 37, No. 1-2, 1997, p. 30.

15. See Richard Wright, *The Color Curtain: A Report on the Bandung Conference*, 2nd Ed., Jackson, MS: University Press of Mississippi, 1994.

16. Jawaharlal Nehru, *The Discovery of India*, 1946, New Delhi, India: Oxford University Press, 1994, p. 464.

17. See Christopher Andrew and Vasili Mitrokhin, *The World Was Going Our Way: The KGB and the Battle for the Third World*, New York: Basic Books, 2005, pp. 439-444.

18. See Ajay K. Dubey, "India-Africa State Relations (1972-1997)," *Africa Quarterly*, Vol. 37, No. 1-2, 1997, pp. 43-57.

19. See Thomas and Margaret Melady, *Idi Amin Dada: Hitler in Africa*, Kansas City, KS: Sheed, Andrews & McMeel, 1977, pp. 70-93. (Thomas Melady was the U.S. ambassador to Uganda from 1972 until 1973, when he persuaded the State Department to close the American Embassy in the aftermath of the expulsion of the South Asians.)

20. Salman Haidar, "Focus on Africa: India Gears Up For a More Active Policy," *The Statesman*, July 12, 2007, available from *www.thestatesman.net/page.arcview.php?clid=3&id=189853&usrsess=1.*

21. See Ruchita Beri, "India's Africa Policy in the Post-Cold War Era: An Assessment," *Strategic Analysis*, Vol. 17, No. 2, April-June 2003, pp. 228-229.

22. See Tushdar Poddar and Eva Yi, *India's Rising Growth Potential*, Goldman Sachs Global Economics Paper No. 152, New York: Goldman Sachs, 2007, pp. 9-13.

23. See Dominic Wilson and Roopa Purushothaman, *Dreaming with BRICs: The Path to 2050*, Goldman Sachs Global Economics Paper No. 99, New York: Goldman Sachs, 2003.

24. See Sumit Ganguly and Manjeet S. Pardesi, "India Rising: What is New Delhi to Do?" *World Policy Journal*, Vol. 24, No. 1, Spring 2007, pp. 9-18.

25. For a comparison of the rise of China and India and their prospects, see David Smith, *Growling Tiger, Roaring Dragon: India, China and the New World Order*, Vancouver: Douglas & McIntyre, 2007.

26. See Tanvi Madan, *Brookings Institution Energy Security Series: India*, Washington, DC: Brookings Institution, 2006, pp. 9-13.

27. International Energy Agency, *Oil in India 2006*, available from *www.iea.org/Textbase/stats/oildata.asp?COUNTRY_CODE=IN*.

28. See Nivedita Ray, "Sudan Crisis: Exploring India's Role," *Strategic Analysis*, Vol. 31, No. 1, January/February 2007, pp. 93-109.

29. "India ONGC in Race for Ghana Oilfield Stake—Report," *Reuters*, July 14, 2009, available from *in.reuters.com/article/companyNews/idINBOM48761620090714*.

30. John Mitchell and Glada Lahn, *Oil for Asia*, Chatham House Energy, Environment and Development Programme Briefing Paper, London, UK: Chatham House 2007, p. 9.

31. Rajesh Pillania, "India's Interest in Africa Oil," *Africa Age*, Vol. 1, No. 2, January 2008, p. 35.

32. "Uganda Invites Indian Assistance for Quicker Development of Oil and Gas Sector," Government of India, Press Information Bureau, January 28, 2010, available from *pib.nic.in/release/release.asp?relid=57386*.

33. "India Re-Draws Strategy in African Oil Assets," *The Hindu*, February 7, 2010, available from *beta.thehindu.com/business/article102263.ece*.

34. See Press Trust of India, "JSW Acquires Control of South African Coal Mining Company," *The Hindu*, April 19, 2010, available from *beta.thehindu.com/business/article405286.ece*.

35. "B.K. Birla Firm Close to Buying Tea Estate in Africa," *Business Standard*, November 30, 2009, available from *www.business-standard.com/india/news/b-k-birla-firm-close-to-buying-tea-estate-in-africa/378074/*.

36. Development Centre of the Organisation for Economic Co-operation and Development (OECD), *The Rise of China and India: What's in It for Africa?* Paris, France: OECD, 2006, p. 94.

37. See Dharmendra Rataul, "Farmers to Explore Africa for Agricultural Prospects," *Indian Express*, February 23, 2010, available from *www.indianexpress.com/news/Farmers-to-explore-Africa-for-agriculture-prospects/583144*.

38. See Ajay K. Dubey, "India-Africa Relations: Historical Connections and Recent Trends," in *Trends in Indo-African Relations*, New Delhi, India: Manas, 2010, pp. 35-36.

39. Sushant K. Singh, *India and West Africa: A Burgeoning Relationship*, Chatham House Asia Programme Briefing Paper, London, UK: Chatham House, 2007, p. 6.

40. See Gareth Price, *India's Aid Dynamics: From Recipient to Donor?* Chatham House Asia Programme Working Paper, London, UK: Chatham House, 2004, p. 12.

41. See Parvathi Vasudevan, "Afro-India Economic Relations: Cup—Half Full?" in Dubey, *Trends in Indo-African Relations*, p. 55.

42. See "Government Makes Kalam's Dream Come Alive," *The Hindu*, July 5, 2007, available from *www.hindu.com/thehindu/holnus/002200707051440.htm*. (Thanks to Dr. Ram Narayanan of Pennsylvania State University for originally calling this development to the author's attention.)

43. See Kripa Sridharan, "Commercial Diplomacy and Statecraft in the Context of Economic Reform: The Indian Experience," *Diplomacy & Statecraft*, Vol. 13, No. 2, June 2002, pp. 57-82.

44. See William R. Snyder, "India's Top Vehicle Maker Looks to Africa," *Wall Street Journal*, March 2, 2010, available from *online. wsj.com/article/SB10001424052748703807904575097393425602292. html?mod=WSJ_latestheadlines&mg=com-wsj*.

45. "CII India-Africa Project Partnership Conclave to Generate $17 Billion Business," Confederation of Indian Industry, October 11, 2006, available from *www.ciionline.org/news/news-Main11-10-2006_1.html*.

46. See Human Siddiqi, "India-Africa Summit to Take Up 145 Projects Worth $9 Billion," *Financial Express*, March 11, 2010, available from *www.financialexpress.com/news/India-Africa-summit-to-take-up-145-projects-worth – 9-billion/589246/*.

47. See "500 Indian Companies Invest Five Billion U.S. Dollars in Ethiopia," *Ethiopian News*, April 7, 2010, available from *www.ethiopian-news.com/500-indian-companies-invest-five-billon-us-dollars-in-ethiopia/*.

48. See "Essar Pumps $2 Billion into African Telecoms," *IT News Africa*, February 1, 2010, available from *www.itnewsafrica. com/?p=4463*.

49. See Scott Baldauf, "India Firm Bharti Airtel Goes Big into African Cellphone Market," *Christian Science Monitor*, March 1, 2010, available from *www.csmonitor.com/World/Africa/2010/0303/India-firm-Bharti-Airtel-goes-big-into-African-cellphone-market*.

50. Anand Sharma, quoted in "India's Ties with Africa Distinct from Others," *Indo-Asian News Service*, March 15, 2010, available from *sify.com/finance/india-s-ties-with-africa-distinct-from-others-anand-sharma-news-default-kdprkciabha.html*.

51. There are Indian embassies or high commissions in Algeria, Angola, Botswana, the Democratic Republic of the Congo, Côte d'Ivoire, Egypt, Ethiopia, Ghana, Kenya, Libya, Madagascar, Mali, Mauritius, Morocco, Mozambique, Namibia, Niger, Nigeria, Seychelles, South Africa, Sudan, Tanzania, Tunisia, Uganda, Zambia, and Zimbabwe. Honorary Consulates-General are found in the following countries without a resident diplomatic mission: Benin, Burkina Faso, Cameroon, Chad, Comoros, the Republic of Congo (Brazzaville), Djibouti, Gabon, The Gambia, Guinea, Liberia, Mauritania, Rwanda, Sierra Leone, and Togo.

52. The documents are available from *www.africa-union.org/root/au/Conferences/2008/april/India-Africa/India-Africa.html*,

53. "Indian Government Allocates $6 Billion for Implementation of India-Africa Cooperation Forum Decisions," *Nazret.com*, December 6, 2009, available from *nazret.com/blog/index.php?title=indian_gov_t_allocates_6_bln_usd_for_imp&more=1&c=1&tb=1&pb=1*.

54. Pranab Mukherjee, Address at the Africa Day Lecture on "India Africa Relations," New Delhi, India, May 26, 2010, available from *mea.gov.in/speech/2010/05/26ss01.htm*.

55. See Chris Alden and Marco Antonio Vieira, "The New Diplomacy of the South: South Africa, Brazil, India and Trilateralism," *Third World Quarterly*, Vol. 26, No. 7, 2005, pp. 1077-1095.

56. Agence France-Press, "India, Brazil, South Africa Aim to Boost Trade," July 17, 2007, available from *www.industryweek.com/ReadArticle.aspx?ArticleID=14618*. Also, see Isabel Hofmyer and Michelle Williams, "South Africa-India: Connections and Comparisons," *Journal of Asian and African Studies*, Vol. 44, No. 1, February 2009, pp. 5-17.

57. "African Students Favour India over Europe and U.S.," *Daily News and Analysis*, May 2, 2010, available from *www.dna-india.com/academy/report_african-students-favour-india-over-europe-and-us_1378211*.

58. See "India Offers Fellowships to African Researchers," *Indo-Asian News Service*, February 19, 2010, available from *www.littleabout.com/General/india-offers-fellowships-african-researchers,71822.html*.

59. See Christopher Griffin, "What India Wants," *Armed Forces Journal*, Vol. 143, No. 10, May 2006, pp. 16-18.

60. See Xenia Dormandy, "Is India, or Will It Be, a Responsible International Stakeholder?" *Washington Quarterly*, Vol. 30, No. 3, Summer 2007, pp. 117-130.

61. "UN Liberia Envoy Hails Indian Female Police Unit for Gender Equality Role, Performance," *UN News Centre*, August 20, 2007, available from *www.un.org/apps/news/story.asp?NewsID=235 52&Cr=liberia&Cr1=*.

62. United Nations Peacekeeping, Ranking of Military and Police Contributions to UN Operations, June 30, 2010, available from *www.un.org/en/peacekeeping/contributors/2010/june10_2.pdf*.

63. Specifically, India has 4,247 troops, 305 police, and 48 military observers and other experts with the UN Organization Stabilization Mission in the DRC (MONUSCO); 248 police with the UN Mission in Liberia (UNMIL); 2,637 troops, 46 police, and 18 military observers and other experts with the UN Mission in the Sudan (UNMIS); and 8 military observers and other experts with the UN Operation in Côte d'Ivoire (ONUCI). See United Nations Peacekeeping, UN Missions Summary Detailed by Country, June 30, 2009, available from *www.un.org/en/peacekeeping/contributors/2010/june10_3.pdf*.

64. *Ibid.* With the exception of China, which currently deploys 1,622 personnel to UN peacekeeping operations in Africa, the contributions of the other permanent members of the Security Council are negligible: France (62), the Russian Federation (227), the United Kingdom (7), and the United States (29).

65. See Ruchita Beri, "Indo-South African Defense Cooperation: Potential and Prospects," *Strategic Analysis*, Vol. 23, No. 10, January 2000, pp. 1681-1705; also see Deane-Peter Baker, *New Partnerships for a New Era: Enhancing the South African Army's Stabilization Role in Africa*, Carlisle, PA: Strategic Studies Institute, U.S. Army War College, 2009.

66. See Shalini Chawla, "United Nations Mission in Sierra Leone: A Search for Peace," *Strategic Analysis*, Vol. 24, No. 9, December 2000, pp. 1745-1755; also see J. Peter Pham, *The Sierra Leonean Tragedy: History and Global Dimensions*, New York: Nova Science, 2006, pp. 148-151.

67. See Ruchita Beri, "India's Role in Keeping the Peace in Africa," *Strategic Analysis*, Vol. 32, No. 2, March 2008, pp. 197-221.

68. See J. Peter Pham, "The Failed State and Regional Dimensions of Somali Piracy," in Bibi van Ginkel and Frans-Paul van der Putten, eds., *The International Response to Somali Piracy: Challenges and Opportunities*, Leiden, South Holland: Martinus Nijhoff, 2010, pp. 25-47; also see "Putting Somali Piracy in Context," *Journal of Contemporary African Studies*, Vol. 28, No. 3, July 2010, pp. 325-341.

69. See Brian Wilson, "Naval Diplomacy and Maritime Security in the Western Indian Ocean," *Strategic Analysis*, Vol. 33, No. 4, July 2009, p. 488.

70. See Donald L. Berlin, "India in the Indian Ocean," *Naval War College Review*, Vol. 59, No. 2, Spring 2006, pp. 58-89.

71. See Patrick Mutahi, "India Plays Globo Cop Off Somali Coast as Western Navies Play Safe," *Daily Nation*, December 18, 2008, available from *www.nation.co.ke/News/africa/-/1066/504022/-/view/printVersion/-/u65ioa/-/index.html*.

72. See Manu Pubby, "India Activates First Listening Post on Foreign Soil: Radars in Madagascar," *Indian Express*, July 18, 2007, available from *www.indianexpress.com/news/india-activates-first-listening-post-on-foreign-soil-radars-in-madagascar/205416/*.

73. See Sudha Ramachandran, "India's Quiet Sea Power," *Asia Times*, August 2, 2007, available from *www.atimes.com/atimes/South_Asia/IH02Df01.html*.

74. See Beri, "India's Africa Policy in the Post-Cold War Era," p. 228.

75. National Intelligence Council, *India Defense Industry: Domestic Production and Imports—The Future Balance*, November 15, 2001, available from *www.nti.org/e_research/official_docs/cia/111501CIA.pdf*.

76. Jackie Cowhig, "India Paying Highest Prices for South Africa Coal—Producers," *Reuters*, July 27, 2009, available from *in.reuters.com/article/domesticNews/idINLR21799020090727*.

77. Karen J. Monaghan, "India Offers 'Lesson of Entrepreneurship' to Africa," interview by Stephanie Hanson, *Council on Foreign Relations Audio Brief*, June 29, 2007, available from *www.cfr.org/publication/13701/monaghan.html?breadcrumb=%2Fregion%2F282%2Findia*.

78. See François Lafargue, "Chine et Inde: La ruée, vers le pétrole" ("China and India: Take Off after the Petroleum"), *Enjeux Internationaux*, Vol. 15, 2007, pp. 34-37.

79. Rajiv Sikri, *Challenge and Strategy: Rethinking India's Foreign Policy*, New Delhi, India: Sage, 2009, p. 237.

80. James Shikwati, "Africa, as a New Frontier: Global Competition for Oil and India's Approach," in Ruchita Bero and Uttam Kumar Sinha, eds., *Africa and Energy Security: Global Issues, Local Responses*, New Delhi, India: Academic Foundation, 2009, p. 45.

81. See Dani Rodrick, *From "Hindu Growth" to Productivity Surge: The Mystery of the Indian Growth Transition*, National Bureau of Economic Research Working Paper 5317, Cambridge, MA: NBER, 2004.

82. Prime Minister Manmohan Singh, Speech to the India Today Conclave, February 25, 2005, available from *www.pmindia.nic.in/speech/content.asp?id=78*.

83. Greg Mills, "Reflections: India, IBSA and the IOR," *Strategic Analysis*, Vol. 32, No. 1, January 2008, p. 139.

84. *National Security Strategy of the United States of America*, March 16, 2006, available from *georgewbush-whitehouse.archives.gov/nsc/nss/2006/*.

85. *National Security Strategy of the United States of America*, May 27, 2010, available from *www.whitehouse.gov/sites/default/files/rss_viewer/national_security_strategy.pdf*.

86. Jack Mangala, "Africa and the New World Era: Contexts and Stakes," in Jack Mangala, ed., *Africa and the New World Era: From Humanitarianism to a Strategic View*, New York: Palgrave Macmillan, 2010, p. 9.

87. *Ibid.*

88. See Stephen Blank, "Nuclear Fusion," *Armed Forces Journal*, Vol. 144, No. 7, February 2007, pp. 20-24, 46.

89. Robert D. Blackwill, "The India Imperative," *The National Interest*, No. 80, Summer 2005, p. 9.

90. Henry A. Kissinger, "Working with India," *The Washington Post*, March 20, 2006, p. A15.

91. Hillary Rodham Clinton, Remarks with Indian Minister of External Affairs S.M. Krishna, Washington, DC, June 3, 2010, available from *www.state.gov/secretary/rm/2010/06/142642.htm*.

92. Ashley J. Tellis, Testimony before the Subcommittee on Asia and the Pacific, Committee on International Relations, United States House of Representatives, July 14, 2005, available from *www.fas.org/terrorism/at/docs/2005/aphear_14_jun_05/tellis.pdf*.

93. On U.S. interests in Africa, see J. Peter Pham, "America's New Africa Command: Paradigm Shift or Step Backwards?" *Brown Journal of World Affairs*, Vol. 15, No. 1, Fall/Winter 2008, pp. 257-272; "Been There, Already Doing That: America's Ongoing Security Engagement in Africa," *Contemporary Security Policy*, Vol. 30, No. 1, April 2009, pp. 72-78; and "U.S. Strategic Relations with Africa after 9/11," in Matthew J. Morgan, ed., *The Impact of 9/11: The Day that Changed Everything?* New York: Palgrave Macmillan, 2009, pp. 231-244.

94. In 2004, for example, the PRC used its diplomatic and financial leverage with the government of Angola to get the latter's state-owned oil company, Sonangol, to exercise its preemption rights to prevent a move by India's ONGC to purchase the half-ownership of a major production block from the Anglo-Dutch energy giant Shell. India has yet to achieve significant access to the

Angolan petroleum sector. See Alex Vines, Lillian Wong, Markus Weimer, and Indira Campos, *Thirst for African Oil: Asian National Oil Companies in Nigeria and Angola*, London, UK: Chatham House, 2009.

95. See Princeton N. Lyman, "China Ups the Ante in Africa," in Princeton N. Lyman and Patricia Dorff, eds., *Beyond Humanitarianism: What You Need to Know About Africa and Why It Matters*, New York: Council on Foreign Relations, 2007, pp. 19-22.

96. Griffin, p. 16.

97. See Amit Gupta, *The U.S.-India Relationship: Strategic Partnership or Complementary Interest*, Carlisle, PA: Strategic Studies Institute, U.S. Army War College, 2005, pp. 32-33.

98. Condoleezza Rice, quoted in Lalit Mansingh, *Indo-U.S. Strategic Partnership: Are We There Yet?* New Delhi, India: Institute of Peace and Conflict Studies, 2006, p. 4.

99. Gupta, p. 45.

100. Indo-U.S. Framework for Maritime Security Cooperation, March 2, 2006, available from *www.defense.gov/news/Mar2006/d200600302indo-usframeworkformaritimesecuritycooperation.pdf*.

101. *National Security Strategy of the United States of America*, 2010.

102. U.S. Africa Command, Fact Sheet, "United States Africa Command," October 18, 2008, available from *www.africom.mil/getArticle.asp?art=1644*.

103. Barack Obama, Remarks in Joint Press Conference with Prime Minister Singh of India, Washington, DC, November 24, 2009, available from *www.whitehouse.gov/the-press-office/remarks-president-obama-and-prime-minister-singh-india-joint-press-conference*.

104. Robert D. Blackwill, "A Friend Indeed," *The National Interest*, No. 89, May/June 2007, p. 16.

www.ingramcontent.com/pod-product-compliance
Lightning Source LLC
Chambersburg PA
CBHW060003300526
45794CB00003B/1070